SOCCER'S Greatest Clubs

Paris Saint-Germain FC

Kate Shoup

Cavendish Square
New York

Published in 2020 by Cavendish Square Publishing, LLC
243 5th Avenue, Suite 136, New York, NY 10016

First Edition

Library of Congress Cataloging-in-Publication Data

Names: Shoup, Kate, 1972- author.
Title: Paris Saint-Germain FC / Kate Shoup.
Other titles: Paris Saint-Germain Football Club
Description: First edition. | New York : Cavendish Square, 2020. | Series: Soccer's greatest clubs | Audience: Grades: 5 to 8. | Includes bibliographical references and index.
Identifiers: LCCN 2019016445 (print) | LCCN 2019021835 (ebook) | ISBN 9781502652874 (ebook) | ISBN 9781502652867 (library bound) | ISBN 9781502652850 (pbk.)
Subjects: LCSH: Paris-Saint-Germain-Football-Club--History--Juvenile literature. | Soccer teams--France--Paris--Juvenile literature.
Classification: LCC GV943.6.P37 (ebook) | LCC GV943.6.P37 S47 2020 (print) | DDC 796.334/640944361--dc23
LC record available at https://lccn.loc.gov/2019016445

Editor: Kristen Susienka
Copy Editor: Rebecca Rohan
Associate Art Director: Alan Sliwinski
Designer: Joe Parenteau
Production Coordinator: Karol Szymczuk
Photo Research: J8 Media

The photographs in this book are used by permission and through the courtesy of: Photo credits: Cover Comzeal Images/Shutterstock.com (used throughout), Onur Cem/Shutterstock.com (used throughout), Focus Stocker/Shutterstock.com (used throughout); p. 4 Franck Fife/AFP/Getty Images; p. 6 Lincolnshire County Council, Usher Gallery, Lincoln, UK/Bridgeman Images; p. 8 Faiz Zaki/Shutterstock.com; p. 9 AUGER Benjamin/Getty Images; p. 11 Romain Lafabregue/AFP/Getty Images; p. 12 Print Collector/Getty Images; p. 15 Print Collector/Getty Images; p. 16 Universal/Corbis/VCG/Getty Images; p. 18 Franck Fife/AFP/Getty Images; p. 20 Universal/Corbis/VCG/Getty Images; p. 26 Tim Clayton/Corbis/Getty Images; p. 28 Gerard Bedeau/Onze/Icon Sport/Getty Images; p. 30 Kenzo Tribouillard/AFP/Getty Images; p. 31 Franck Fife/AFP/Getty Images; p. 33 Aurelien Meunier/Getty Images; p. 36 PA Images/Alamy Stock Photo; p. 38 Trabantos/Shutterstock.com; p. 39 Franck Fife/AFP/Getty Images; p. 41 Ricochet64/Shutterstock.com; p. 44 Michael Regan/Getty Images; p. 46 Jean Catuffe/Getty Images; p. 48 Franck Fife/AFP/Getty Images; p. 49 Fred Dufour/AFP/Getty Images; p. 50 Marc Lecureuil/PSG/SIPA/Newscom; p. 52 Jean Catuffe/Getty Images.

Printed in the United States of America

TABLE OF CONTENTS

Paris Saint-Germain players celebrate after winning the Coupe de la Ligue in 2014. This is a competition played between all other league teams. The team that wins the trophy, or cup, is the best team in the league.

1

INTRODUCING PARIS SAINT-GERMAIN

Paris Saint-Germain Football Club (FC) is a famous soccer team in France. It has been around since 1970. Soccer is a very popular sport around the world. It is a ball game played by two teams with eleven players on each side. They play on a large rectangular field called a pitch. The pitch has a goal on each end.

One player is called the goalie. The goalie's job is to protect his or her team's goal. Only goalies are allowed to touch the ball with their hands when it is in play. Other players must move the ball by kicking it with their feet or by using their legs, knees, chest, or head.

The object of soccer is to put the ball in the other team's goal. The team that scores the most goals before time runs out wins. If both teams have the same number of goals when time runs out, then the match will usually end in a draw, or tie. However, if the match is part of a knockout tournament, then it will go into overtime. In overtime, the teams play the game for thirty more minutes. If the game is still tied after overtime, it will go to a shootout. In a shootout, both teams pick five players. Each player has one chance to shoot a goal directly into the net, with only the goalie to keep it from going in. This is called a penalty kick. Whichever team scores the most penalty kicks during a shootout wins the game.

THE HISTORY OF SOCCER

Nobody knows exactly how soccer started. People in ancient China played a game that involved kicking a ball around, and so did people in ancient Greece. Other countries around the world, such as Scotland and England, also liked similar kinds of games.

Modern soccer grew out of another popular sport called rugby football. That sport combined parts of what we now call soccer with what we now call rugby.

People in England have played games similar to soccer for centuries.

SPORT SHORT

The word soccer is an abbreviation of the word "association" (socc) plus the suffix "-er."

People organized teams, called sports clubs. In 1863, representatives from several sports clubs in London, England, met to come up with the rules of soccer. They also created a new group to govern the game. It was called the Football Association (FA). The sport became known as "association football" or just "football." (This was to set it apart from rugby football.) Only people in the United States and a few other countries call it "soccer" today.

PARIS SAINT-GERMAIN BEGINS

Englishmen living in Paris, France, started the first soccer team in that country in 1863. Soon, more clubs formed. They were organized into regional leagues. By the early 1900s, there were nearly three hundred soccer clubs in France. There were ten of these around Paris alone. One of these was a club called Stade Saint-Germain. It was started in 1904. Like all clubs at that time, it was an amateur, or nonprofessional, club.

Soccer became even more popular in France after World War I. A French professional soccer league was started in 1932. It was called Ligue 1. By the late 1960s, only one team from Paris qualified to play in Ligue 1. A group of businessmen from Paris wanted to change that. In 1969, they started a new team called Paris Football Club (FC). In 1970, Paris FC merged with Stade

SPORT SHORT

Stade Saint-Germain started during the Belle Époque (Beautiful Era). It was a time of optimism and prosperity in France.

Saint-Germain. This new team was called Paris Saint-Germain Football Club, or PSG for short.

During its first season (1970–1971), PSG played in a lower-level league called Ligue 2. The next year, it was promoted, or allowed to move up, to Ligue 1.

Paris Saint-Germain Football Club was formed in 1970. The logo today pays tribute to the club's founding.

Then, disaster struck. Faced with financial problems, the team had no choice but to split in two. Half of the team became Paris FC. It was allowed to stay in Ligue 1. The other half kept the name Paris Saint-Germain. It was demoted, or brought down, to an amateur league called the Championnat National, or Division 3.

LIGUE 1 AND CHAMPIONS LEAGUE

In just two seasons the "new" PSG clawed its way back into Ligue 1. It has played in that league ever since. It has won more major championships, or competitions, than any other team in Ligue 1. PSG also frequently qualifies to play in an international league called the Champions League. The Champions League is a yearly tournament played by professional teams throughout Europe. The winner of the Champions League is

The 1977–1978 Paris Saint-Germain squad poses for a picture. Team manager Daniel Hechter, who designed the team's jerseys, is on the far right.

PSG: THE YOUNG UPSTART

Paris Saint-Germain is one of the newer clubs in Ligue 1. Some Ligue 1 clubs were started in the late 1800s. That makes PSG's success even more impressive. It has had fewer chances to win major championships but has still won more than any other French team.

considered the top team in Europe. PSG has never won the Champions League tournament as of 2019.

FRANCE'S TOP CLUB

In 2011, a company called Oryx Qatar Sports Investments (QSi) bought PSG. QSi is located in Qatar, a wealthy oil-producing nation in the Middle East.

QSi put a lot of money into Paris Saint-Germain. This allowed PSG to get more top players from around the world to join the team. These included a young Brazilian named Neymar da Silva Santos Júnior and a French teenager called Kylian Mbappé. Since QSi bought PSG, it has become the all-time top club in France. PSG is also France's wealthiest team. It makes more money than any other professional team in France.

"DREAM BIGGER"

After QSi bought PSG, the club made up a new slogan, or saying, called "Dream Bigger." PSG's dream is to become one of the biggest teams in sports. The team wants to be equal to other top European soccer clubs, like Manchester United in England or Real Madrid and Barcelona in Spain.

To reach this goal, the team will need to do better in the Champions League. It has never made it past the quarterfinal stage. In 2019, it was knocked out by Manchester United in a match PSG was predicted to win. However, because the squad is very talented and management can bring good players to the team, PSG could win the Champions League in the future.

Paris Saint-Germain players applaud after a game against Olympique Lyonnais in 2019.

Soldiers in the French Army enjoyed playing football, as shown in this poster from 1902.

STARTING A CLUB

2

Soccer arrived in France in the early 1860s. By the early 1900s, there were many clubs in the Paris area, but Paris Saint-Germain wasn't started until 1970.

THE BIRTH OF SOCCER IN FRANCE

The first known soccer club in France was founded in 1863 by a group of Englishmen living in Paris. They played their matches in a famous Parisian park called the Bois de Boulogne. It was a casual, or nonprofessional, club.

Soon, more serious clubs emerged. The first was Le Havre Athletic Club (AC). It was started in 1872 in a French city called Le Havre. Most Le Havre AC players were English sailors. At first, the club played a version of soccer that was part rugby football and part association football (what we think of as soccer). In 1894, it switched to association football only.

French soccer grew in popularity. Regional leagues developed. In 1894, a group called the Union des Sociétés Françaises de Sports Athlétiques (USFSA) organized the first-ever French soccer championship. It was a knockout tournament. A team from Paris called Standard Athletic Club won. In 1904, the USFSA put together a French national team for the first time. In 1919, the USFSA was replaced by another organization: the Fédération Française de Football, or French Football Federation (FFF). The FFF still runs French soccer today.

In 1904, another important soccer organization was started in France. It was called the Fédération Internationale de Football Association (FIFA). Its purpose was—and still is—to govern, or manage, international soccer competitions.

WORLD WAR I AND THE GROWTH OF FRENCH SOCCER

By 1906, there were 270 soccer clubs in France. Most of these were in rich cities in the northern part of the country.

Soccer was less popular in the south and poor rural, or country, areas. People in these places were suspicious about soccer because it was an English sport. There is a long history of France and England not getting along. Besides, few people in these areas had time for sports. They were busy taking care of their land.

French attitudes about soccer improved during and after World War I. Many French soldiers fought alongside British soldiers during the war. After a while, the British soldiers began challenging French soldiers in soccer matches and even organizing tournaments. After

French soldiers are shown here marching during World War I. Many soldiers learned how to play soccer during the war.

the war, when French soldiers returned home, they brought soccer with them.

THE START OF STADE SAINT-GERMAIN

On June 21, 1904, a new soccer club was started in a Paris suburb called Saint-Germain-en-Laye. The new club was called Stade Saint-Germain. Stade Saint-Germain joined the USFSA. It played in a regional league called the Division d'Honneur (DH) de la Ligue de Paris (Honor Division of the Paris League). The club was led by a man named Félix Boyer.

The 1970 Paris Saint-Germain squad lined up for this photo. This was the first squad to play for Paris Saint-Germain.

Stade Saint-Germain was an amateur club. It won the DH de la Ligue de Paris title in 1957. After winning this title, the club was promoted to a national league called the Championnat de France Amateurs (CFA). Stade Saint-Germain did not do well in the CFA. Just three years after its promotion, Stade Saint-Germain was relegated—sent back—to the DH de la Ligue de Paris.

In 1969, the club reached the quarterfinals in an important national tournament called the Coupe de France (French Cup). The Coupe de France was first played in 1917. It is an annual tournament that is open to all amateur and professional soccer clubs in France. It is organized by the FFF. Advancing to the quarterfinals was a big deal for Stade Saint-Germain.

Stade Saint-Germain was just one of hundreds of small amateur teams in France. In 1970, Stade Saint-Germain would become famous when it merged with another team to form Paris Saint-Germain.

PROFESSIONAL SOCCER IN FRANCE

In 1932, the FFF started a professional league. This league became known as Ligue 1.

In its first season, Ligue 1 had twenty teams from all over France. The twenty Ligue 1 teams were divided into two groups of ten, which can be referred to as Group A and Group B. Each team in Group A played every other team in Group A in a round-robin format. Teams earned three points for each win, one point for each tie, and zero points for each loss. The team with the most points won Group A. The same went for Group B. Then, the winner of Group A played the winner of Group B in a final to decide the league champion. A team called Olympique Lillois from the city of Lille was the first-ever champion of Ligue 1. The next season, the FFF started a second professional league, called Ligue 2. Ligue 2 was one level below Ligue 1.

Over the years, the number of clubs in each league changed. Eventually, the FFF decided that both leagues would have twenty clubs each. The group format also

SPORT SHORT

The Ligue 1 trophy is called L'Hexagoal. It is shaped like a hexagon. The team that wins L'Hexagoal is considered champion of France.

Paris Saint-Germain midfielder Adrien Rabiot dribbles the ball during the 2018 Coupe de la Ligue final. Paris Saint-Germain went on to win.

went away. Instead, both leagues used a straight round-robin format. Each team in a league played every other team in that same league twice per season—thirty-eight matches in all. They used the same point system as before. The team with the most points at the end of the season—from August to May—was crowned league champion and awarded the league trophy. The same setup is in place today.

Ligue 1 and Ligue 2 use a system of promotion and relegation. At the end of the season, the two teams with the worst records in Ligue 1 are relegated to Ligue 2 for the next season. Meanwhile, the two teams with the best records in Ligue 2 are promoted to Ligue 1. Finally, the team that finishes third-to-last (eighteenth) in Ligue 1 plays a two-match series against the team that finishes third overall in Ligue 2. The winner of that series earns a spot in Ligue 1. The loser must play in Ligue 2.

Clubs in Ligue 1 and Ligue 2 play in an important knockout tournament called the Coupe de la Ligue (French League Cup). A third professional league also participates in the Coupe de la Ligue: the Championnat National. The Championnat National is one level below Ligue 2. Another important championship is the Trophée des Champion. This is a match played by the winner of Ligue 1 and the winner of the Coupe de France.

THE CREATION OF A EUROPEAN LEAGUE SYSTEM

In addition to playing in Ligue 1, some French soccer clubs participate in the international league called the Champions League. It is a season-long tournament run by a soccer group called the Union of European Football Associations (UEFA). UEFA started in 1955 to

SPORT SHORT

Ligue 1 play temporarily stopped during World War II when the Nazis took over France.

DANIEL HECHTER

Fashion designer Daniel Hechter served as club president of Paris Saint-Germain during the 1970s.

In 1973, PSG made an odd choice for club president: a French fashion designer named Daniel Hechter. Hechter was one of the first financial backers of PSG. Some say he cofounded the club. Hechter had also designed the club's crest—its symbol or logo—and its first jersey. The jersey's colors are blue, red, and white—reminding people of the French flag. Its design changes every year, but usually it's a dark blue color with a red stripe down the middle. The players wear a different jersey when they play games away from their home stadium.

Hechter was a key reason PSG became successful. Under Hechter—who was born in Paris in 1938—the team hired top coach Just Fontaine, signed several key players, and got into Ligue 1.

Hechter served as club president for five years. Then, in January 1978, the FFF banned Hechter from soccer for life. They accused him of selling match tickets for more than they were worth and using the money to sign more players. Today, Hechter focuses on his fashion business instead of on soccer.

govern the many national soccer associations in Europe, including the FFF.

The first Champions League tournament was in 1956. Back then, it was called the European Cup. The idea behind the European Cup was to find out which soccer club in Europe was the best. Sixteen teams played in the first European Cup. These included one team from France, Stade de Reims. (It finished second.) Later, the field was expanded to thirty-two teams.

Teams must qualify to play in the Champions League. Some qualify by winning a series of special matches. Most qualify by finishing well in their national league. UEFA ranks the various national leagues to determine how many teams from each league will qualify for the Champions League. For the 2018–2019 Champions League season, Ligue 1 was ranked fifth. It was allowed to send its top three teams into the competition—including Paris Saint-Germain.

The Champions League tournament starts with a round-robin stage and ends with a knockout stage. During the round-robin stage, UEFA divides the thirty-two qualifying teams into eight groups of four. Each team in a group plays all the other teams in that same group—again earning three points for each win, one point for each tie, and zero points for each loss. The two teams with the most points in each group go on to a knockout round of sixteen teams.

UEFA also manages a league called the Europa League. This league is one level below the Champions League. It has a similar format. Many teams that don't make it to the Champions League play in the Europa

League instead. Paris Saint-Germain has played nine seasons in the Europa League.

REVIVING SOCCER IN PARIS

During the early 1900s, Paris had ten soccer clubs. By the late 1960s, that was no longer the case. Several of the city's teams had gone out of business. Only one Parisian team played in Ligue 1: Red Star Football Club, but it seemed Red Star was always near the bottom of the league standings. Paris was one of the only European capitals with no top soccer team.

In January 1969, a group of Parisian businessmen partnered with the FFF to try to start a new elite, or top-level, soccer club in Paris. To see how such a club might be received, they started a petition. A petition is something people sign to say they agree with an idea. If a lot of people signed the petition, it meant a lot of people wanted a new club in the city. The petition got twenty thousand signatures. It seemed that Paris was eager for a new team. In August 1969, the group started a new team called Paris Football Club (FC).

Officials at Paris FC wanted to enter Ligue 1 for the 1970–1971 season. To do this, the team needed players, a stadium in which to play games, and permission from the league to enter. It had none of these, so Paris FC decided to see about joining an existing Ligue 1 club.

None of the top teams wanted to merge, or join, with Paris FC, so Paris FC looked to a lower team. It set its sights on Stade Saint-Germain. The club didn't have a great stadium, but it had players—even some professional ones. Also, thanks to its performance in the 1969 Coupe de France, in which it reached the

LE CLASSIQUE

Paris Saint-Germain FC's main Ligue 1 rival is another top team: Olympique de Marseille (OM). OM is one of the most successful soccer clubs in French history. It has won nine Ligue 1 titles, ten Coupe de France trophies, and one Champions League title as of 2019.

"Marseille versus Paris isn't only a rivalry born from football [soccer] or geography," says soccer journalist Liam Newman. "It is also a war of the classes." In this "war," Paris represents the upper levels of French society while Marseille stands for the working class. These cultural differences make games between the two teams even more exciting.

Any match played between these two teams is called Le Classique (The Classic). Le Classique is considered to be the biggest rivalry in French league play. It is also the most violent. Fans often get into fights. Injuries, arrests, at least one fire (inside the Parc des Princes, where PSG plays), and the death of one PSG fan (in 2010) have all happened during the games.

quarterfinals, it had earned a spot in Ligue 2. It would have to do.

THE BIRTH OF PARIS SAINT-GERMAIN

In August 1970, FC Paris and Stade Saint-Germain officially merged to create a new team: Paris Saint-Germain Football Club. It was just in time for the 1970–1971 Ligue 2 season.

The Paris FC side made sure there was money for club operations, a new stadium, and some new players. These included the captain, or lead player, of the French national team, Jean Djorkaeff. The Stade Saint-Germain side brought many good players and coaches and a place for the team to train.

The merger was immediately successful. PSG won the Ligue 2 championship in its very first year and was promoted to Ligue 1 for the 1971–1972 season. The team's debut, or first, Ligue 1 season was less impressive, however. It finished sixteenth overall—barely escaping relegation.

PSG also had financial, or money-related, problems. The city of Paris offered to pay money to get the team out of trouble—if the team dropped Saint-Germain from its name. The city felt like this would make the team sound more Parisian. The Stade Saint-Germain side of the team was very angry. They refused. There was only one solution: to split PSG into two teams. One team kept the name Paris Saint-Germain. The other took the name Paris Football Club (FC) and the money offered from the city of Paris.

French soccer officials allowed only one team to remain in Ligue 1. That honor—along with all of PSG's professional players—went to Paris FC. The officials demoted PSG not to Ligue 2 but to the Championnat National (then called Division 3). It also stripped the club of its professional status.

STARTING OVER

Paris Saint-Germain played well enough during the 1972–1973 season to earn the second spot in the Division 3 league standings—just missing promotion to Ligue 2. Then, the team that won the Division 3 title shut down. This meant PSG would be promoted to Ligue 2 after all.

For the 1973–1974 season, PSG got a new coach: French soccer legend Just Fontaine. Under Fontaine's leadership, the squad finished second in Ligue 2. As a result, PSG was promoted to Ligue 1 for the 1974–1975 season. The 1973–1974 season was also the first season during which the squad played in its own new stadium, Parc des Princes. It is still the team's home today.

As PSG got better, Paris FC got worse. The year PSG was promoted to Ligue 1, Paris FC was relegated to Ligue 2. It returned to Ligue 1 in 1978 but for one season only. During the 1980s, the squad struggled even more. It dropped as low as Division 4—an amateur league. It currently plays in Ligue 2. As of 2019, Paris FC has not returned to France's top league since 1979.

Kylian Mbappé (*left*) celebrates with teammate Juan Bernat after scoring the winning goal in a match against Toulouse FC in 2019.

3 HIGHS AND LOWS

Paris Saint-Germain's history has been a series of highs and lows. In recent years, the club has seen incredible success. New owners have put a lot of money into the team to bring top soccer stars from around the world to PSG.

BUILDING A ROSTER OF STARS

During the 1970s, Paris Saint-Germain Football Club slowly built up a list, or roster, of star players. One of the first was a midfielder from Algeria named Mustapha Dahleb. Dahleb played from 1974 to 1984. Another was Argentine sensation Carlos Bianchi. He played at the forward, or striker, position from 1977 to 1979. A midfielder named Dominique Bathenay and a winger called Dominique Rocheteau soon followed. Bathenay played from 1978 to 1985 and Rocheteau from 1980 to 1987. Spanish defender and midfielder Luis Fernández also arrived in 1978. He played until 1986. Finally, a Yugoslavian midfielder named Safet Sušić, who played from 1982 to 1991, and French goalie Joël Bats, who

Algerian midfielder Mustapha Dahleb played for Paris Saint-Germain from 1974 to 1984.

played from 1985 to 1992, rounded out the squad in the team's early years.

A CYCLE OF DECLINE AND REVIVAL

The late 1970s were building years for PSG. In 1982, all that effort paid off. The team won its first-ever major trophy: the Coupe de France. It won the Coupe again the very next year. In 1986, PSG claimed its first-ever Ligue 1 title. PSG also qualified for international play for the first time during this period. It competed in the UEFA Europa League in 1984–1985 and the UEFA Champions League in 1986–1987.

Then, a drought happened. Between 1986 and 1991, the team sank in the standings—and its finances sank with it. Finally, a television company called Canal+ bought the team in 1991. It cleared the team's debts and hired a new coach named Artur Jorge, who was from Portugal. Over the next few years, it also brought in several new players. One of these was Liberian forward George Weah (1992–1995). Another was Brazilian midfielder Raí (1993–1998).

PSG quickly returned to form. The early 1990s brought a string of successes. Between 1991 and 1999, the club finished in the top three in Ligue 1 play seven times—including a first-place finish in 1993–1994. PSG also won the Coupe de France three times, the Coupe de la Ligue twice, and the Trophée des Champions once. In 1996, it claimed its first-ever international championship: the European Cup Winners' Cup. This tournament was played by the winners of all European domestic cup competitions.

These winning ways would not last, however. In the late 1990s, the team once again started to decline due to mismanagement. It fell deep into debt. One by one, its top players left. Between 2000 and 2011, the team hovered near the bottom of the Ligue 1 standings. It was nearly relegated in 2007–2008.

UNDER NEW OWNERSHIP

In 2007, Canal+ split from PSG. It sold the club to a group of investment firms for €41 million, or $46 million. The club was sold again in 2011–2012, this time to a group called Oryx Qatar Sports Investments (QSi) for €80 million ($89 million). It has been said that then–French president Nicolas Sarkozy had a hand in the deal. (Sarkozy is a PSG supporter.)

QSi bought PSG for one simple reason. London has six soccer clubs capable of competing in international play. Other European cities, such as Milan, Madrid, and even Manchester, have two. In these cities, the fan base is spread among multiple teams. This is not so in Paris. Paris has a population of twelve million, but it has only one elite soccer club. That club—and its league—was ripe for development. Growth potential aside, Paris is one of the world's most wonderful and glamorous cities. QSi chairman Nasser al-Khelaïfi acknowledged that "the location of the club in Paris, a leading capital of the world, was very important" in QSi's decision to buy PSG.

PSG quickly announced its new slogan: "Dream Bigger." It was something QSi took to heart. "In five years, we want to be one of the best clubs in Europe and to win the Champions League. And our brand to be worth €1 billion [$1.12 billion]," al-Khelaïfi told a reporter in 2014. Al-Khelaïfi is the current president of PSG in addition to being chairman of QSi.

To achieve this goal, PSG went on a €302 million ($340 million) spending spree to buy top players from all over the world. In 2012, the club signed a top Brazilian defender named Thiago Silva and a powerful Swedish striker called Zlatan Ibrahimović. In 2013, the team added Uruguayan striker Edinson Cavani and British winger David Beckham. In 2014, it recruited Brazilian defender David Luiz.

In 2017, the team added two more stars. The first was a young Brazilian forward called Neymar. PSG snatched him from another top team: Barcelona. This involved a record-breaking transfer fee of €222 million ($249 million). A transfer fee is a fee paid by a team to get a player who is under contract with another club. This fee is paid in addition to the player's salary.

President of Paris Saint-Germain Nasser al-Khelaïfi (*left*) speaks with former French president—and club supporter—Nicolas Sarkozy (*right*).

The second star was a young French soccer sensation named Kylian Mbappé—also a forward.

PSG initially got Mbappé on loan from a club called AC Monaco. Later, PSG hired the young player—a Paris native—outright after paying a transfer fee of €180 million ($202 million). "For any young person from the Paris region, it is often a dream to wear the red and blue jersey [of PSG] and experience the unique atmosphere of the Parc des Princes," Mbappé said after signing with the club.

Neymar (*left*) and Kylian Mbappé (*right*) celebrate after Paris Saint-Germain's 2018 Coupe de France win.

It used to be that "quality players would typically make a name in France and then leave for fame and fortune in England or Spain," says *New York Times* journalist Sam Borden. That's no longer true. These days, soccer stars are sticking around as PSG works to "become a European powerhouse akin to Real Madrid and Manchester United."

SUCCESS WITH A NEW SQUAD

Soon after QSi took over PSG, the team returned to form. "In less than three years, a mediocre club became a European powerhouse," journalist Hugh Schofield wrote in 2014. "Maybe not up to the Madrids and the Manchesters, but not far behind."

In 2012–2013, PSG won Ligue 1 for the third time. This would be the first of four titles in a row. Although the team fell to the second spot in 2016–2017, it reclaimed top honors in 2017–2018 and remained at the top of the standings for the 2018–2019 season. The QSi era also brought four consecutive Coupe de France titles (2014 to 2018), five consecutive Coupe de la Ligue titles (2014 to 2018), and six consecutive Trophées des Champions (2013 to 2018).

Although the squad has fallen short of its goal to win a Champions League title as of 2019, it has qualified to play in the Champions League several times in the years since QSi took over. Also, it has made it to the quarterfinals in a few seasons in recent years. Before that, the team had qualified only six times in forty-two years. The team has also qualified for the Europa League eight times in its forty-eight-year history but has never won a title.

AWARD-WINNING PLAYERS

Soccer is a team sport, but sometimes individual players really shine. To recognize these players, the soccer world gives out various awards.

SPORT SHORT

Only one French team has ever won a Champions League title: Olympique de Marseille, in 1993.

THE PARIS SAINT-GERMAIN FÉMININES

Marie-Laure Delie is the top all-time scorer for the Paris Saint-Germain Féminines.

Paris Saint-Germain also has a women's team. It is called the PSG Féminines.

The PSG Féminines started in 1971. Between 1971 and 2001, the team played mostly in the Division 2 Féminine league (similar to Ligue 2) with occasional promotions to Division 1 Féminine (similar to Ligue 1). In 2000–2001, the club won the Division 2 title. Since then, it has played exclusively in Division 1. As of 2019, it has won two Coupes de France Féminine, in 2010 and 2018.

In 2011, the team qualified for the UEFA Women's Champions League for the first time ever. It has since qualified four more times as of 2019. The team has gone as far as the semifinals but has never won a Women's Champions League title.

The top all-time goal scorer for Les Féminines is named Marie-Laure Delie. She has played for the team twice, in 2007–2008 and from 2017 to 2018. She scored a total of 131 goals. Other successful players who have worn the PSG Féminines jersey in recent seasons are Lindsey Horan, Irene Paredes, Wang Shuang, and Marie-Antoinette Katoto. All four were on the Guardian's top 100 list of best women soccer players in 2018. In 2019, sixteen players on the team were called to play for their national teams in the run-up to the 2019 Women's World Cup.

Perhaps the most important individual award in soccer is the Ballon d'Or (Golden Ball). This award is given each year by a popular French weekly newspaper called *France Football* to the top player in Europe. The winner is based on a vote by soccer journalists. So far, only one PSG player has won this award: George Weah, in 1995. In 2017, though, Neymar finished third in the voting. PSG could someday soon have a player finish in the top spot.

Mbappé hasn't won a Ballon d'Or yet, but he has won two other important trophies—both for being the top player under the age of twenty-one. The first was the Golden Boy. It's given out by an Italian newspaper called *Tuttosport*. Mbappé won the Golden Boy in 2017. The second was the Kopa Trophy. Like the Ballon d'Or, it's awarded by *France Football*. Mbappé won it in 2018.

PSG players have also been recognized by Ligue 1 on several occasions. Six players have won the Player of the Season award. These include recent squad members Zlatan Ibrahimović (in 2013, 2014, and 2016), Edinson Cavani (in 2017), and Neymar (in 2018). Also, four players have won the Ligue 1 Golden Boot—given to the player who scores the most goals in a season. These include Ibrahimović (again, in 2013, 2014, and 2016) and Cavani (in 2017 and 2018).

SPORT SHORT

After a successful career in soccer, George Weah became the president of the country of Liberia.

THE PARIS SAINT-GERMAIN FOUNDATION

In September 2000, PSG started the Paris Saint-Germain Foundation. The foundation has three key goals. The first goal is to train young people so that they can succeed at work and in life. The second goal is to have after-school programs for children in need. The third goal is to make sick children happy. To do this, the foundation sends players to hospitals throughout Paris to visit sick kids. It also invites sick kids to the club's stadium to meet players there.

Since the foundation started, more than 220,000 children and young adults have been helped by its programs in France and in other countries around the world. "Our aim is for the foundation to continue growing and to reach out to more and more children, inspiring them, giving them the desire and the means to succeed," says Christine Le Gal, who runs the foundation.

Paris Saint-Germain FC has millions of fans around the world.

4

DEALING WITH CHALLENGES

Paris Saint-Germain has become the most successful soccer squad in French history. It has won more major championships than any other French team. However, there have also been some challenges along the way.

FINANCIAL IRREGULARITIES

PSG has faced financial challenges over the years. However, these days, money is not a problem for PSG. In 2019, it had the highest revenues of any club in France and the seventh highest of any soccer club anywhere. In 2018, the club earned €486 million ($529 million). The top-earning teams in 2018 were Manchester United at €682 million ($737 million), Real Madrid at €680 million ($735 million), and Barcelona at €653 million ($706 million).

If anything, the club's problem is that it has—and spends—too much money. Most of this money goes to adding great players to the club's player roster. Some people think PSG has broken UEFA rules that limit spending. These are called financial fair play (FFP) rules. One FFP rule states that a team cannot spend more money than it brings in. UEFA created this FFP rule to keep teams from buying all the top (and most expensive) players and going into debt. People also said that one of PSG's sponsors gave the team too much money. A sponsor is a company that pays money to a team. In return, the sponsor gets to use the team for advertising purposes.

In 2014, UEFA looked into these problems. They agreed that PSG had broken FFP rules. As a punishment

The UEFA headquarters are located in Nyon, Switzerland.

PSG SPONSORS

An airline called Emirates was Paris Saint-Germain's shirt sponsor from 2006 to 2019.

Sponsorship helps any sports team survive—including PSG. It brings the club money and helps build a good reputation with the club. Growing relationships with sponsors is a challenge a club always faces.

An airline called Emirates was PSG's main shirt sponsor from 2006 to 2019. Emirates Air is in the Middle Eastern country of Dubai. Starting in 2019–2020, the shirt sponsor became a hotel company called AccorHotels. This means the AccorHotels logo was put on every PSG player's jersey. AccorHotels owns more than four thousand hotels in over one hundred countries.

PSG is sponsored by other top companies too. Nike provides the club's uniform, or kit. Nike has sponsored PSG since 1989. The Qatari National Bank and a cell phone service provider called Ooredoo are two more main PSG sponsors. Smaller companies also have sponsorship deals with the team, including cell phone service provider Orange, a cell phone maker called Ericsson, a French car company called Renault, and a television network called BEIN Sports. All of these sponsors give PSG money.

for breaking these rules, UEFA fined PSG, or forced it to pay, €60 million ($77 million). UEFA also forced PSG to lower the number of players on its roster and to limit spending over the next two seasons.

PSG went through something similar in 2018. This was after the club spent €222 million ($249 million) to sign Neymar and €180 million ($202 million) to sign Kylian Mbappé. To make sure PSG hadn't spent more money on these players than FFP rules allowed, UEFA started an investigation. However, this time it determined that PSG had not broken FFP rules.

GROWING SOCCER THROUGHOUT FRANCE

Following FFP rules has been one challenge. Another has been turning Paris into a "soccer town" and growing the popularity of soccer throughout France.

It used to be that Parisians paid little attention to soccer. "In Paris, football [soccer] was looked down on by the middle class and the intellectuals," says soccer sportscaster Darren Tulett. Journalist Simon Kuper agrees. "Paris was never a football [soccer] city," he says. "You could spend your life in Paris and never know that football [soccer] existed."

SPORT SHORT

One nickname for PSG is Les Parisiens (The Parisians). Another is Les Rouge-et-Bleu (The Red-and-Blues).

SPORT SHORT

The PSG badge, or crest, has a blue circle with a red drawing of the Eiffel Tower and a small gold flower called a fleur-de-lis.

It wasn't just Paris. People all over France tended to ignore soccer. "There's a slight phenomenon of snobbery around soccer in France," says Duke University history professor Laurent Dubois. The game was far more popular in countries like Spain, England, Italy, and Germany.

PSG is trying to change that, and so far, it's working. The club's successes in the twenty-first century have attracted millions of new fans from all over France. "Thanks to PSG's success, everyone is coming out of the woodwork and declaring themselves to be a fan," says Tulett. "Times have changed," says Kuper. "When there's a big game, Parisians fill cafes to watch on TV."

As PSG has become more popular, it has helped other Ligue 1 teams as well. This is because more TV channels around the world have started to show league play. More TV time means more fans. More importantly, money from showing rights (also called broadcast rights) goes to all teams in Ligue 1—not just PSG. With this money, even teams in smaller French cities will be able to get top players from around the world. This is important. If PSG continues to dominate, or take over, the league, the team might not have competition. Not having competition could be dangerous. "If PSG has such an advantage, the competition doesn't really exist and there is no drama," says former French soccer star Lilian Thuram. "Without drama, people lose interest."

HANDLING HOOLIGANISM

PSG has worked hard to get more fans in Paris and throughout France. However, there's one group of fans the club was forced to let go: the Boulogne Boys. This band of rowdy fans, also called hooligans, was known for its disruptive and even violent behavior during matches. Hooliganism is a common problem for many soccer clubs—not just PSG.

The Boulogne Boys began attending PSG matches during the 1980s. Most of the group's founding members were white supremacists. A white supremacist is a racist person. White supremacists wrongly believe that white people are better than everyone else. The Boulogne Boys shouted rude and racist chants and made fun of the team's nonwhite players. Sometimes, they even got violent.

In response to the Boulogne Boys, a second fan group formed called the Supras Auteuil. Its members were people who were against racism. Many were immigrants or the children of immigrants. Members of the Supras Auteuil got into many fights with the Boulogne Boys. PSG officials did not get involved because they were afraid of being hurt by the groups if they did.

Things changed after one fan died in 2010. PSG banned all fan groups from the Parc des Princes—including the Boulogne Boys and the Supras Auteuil. It also introduced random seating to stop hooligans from gathering in the stadium and increased the cost of tickets so some hooligans couldn't afford to buy them. These changes seemed to make the groups disappear. These days, "the old Boulogne and Auteuil gangs have been reduced to occasional nostalgic scuffles in bars," says Kuper.

Not having these groups in the Parc des Princes made the stadium safer, but it also changed the stadium's atmosphere. Some say it's made the atmosphere worse. Before their ban, "Parc des Princes was one of the most intimidating stadiums to visit in Europe," says soccer journalist Jonathan Johnson. "It would be difficult for teams to play PSG away from home, while the hosts would draw on the energy of their fans and often perform better than the sum of their parts." However, others like the stadium's friendlier feeling.

A DIFFICULT TIME

Some say PSG has gone too far in its attempts to keep hooligans out. The club has been accused of banning not only violent hooligans but "any fan who expresses an opinion that threatens PSG or QSi's commercial interests," says journalist Alexander Shea. Some fans inside the Parc des Princes were banned simply for complaining about ticket prices too loudly. Other fans on social media were threatened with legal action because they criticized the team online.

Later, it was discovered that PSG was keeping dossiers, or detailed notes, on some fans. The team illegally collected personal information on thousands of fans to try to guess who might be a problem during

CHAMPIONS LEAGUE RIVALS

Here, Paris Saint-Germain plays against Barcelona in the 2017 Champions League round of sixteen. Barcelona is Paris Saint-Germain's chief Champions League rival.

Olympique de Marseille is PSG's main rival in Ligue 1, but in the Champions League, Fútbol Club (FC) Barcelona is PSG's chief rival. This rivalry is often seen as a one-sided one. This is because Barcelona is historically a much stronger team. In addition to winning six of eight matches against PSG, Barcelona has won five Champions League titles. In contrast, PSG has never advanced beyond the quarterfinal in Champions League play as of 2019. Therefore, while PSG might focus a lot of energy on Barcelona, Barcelona usually focuses its energy elsewhere—mainly on its archnemesis, Real Madrid.

On occasion, PSG has defeated Barcelona—at least off the field. It has done this by taking top players. One such player was Neymar. PSG signed Neymar from Barcelona in 2017. Another was a young player on Barcelona's junior, or youth, team named Kays Ruiz. As PSG continues to grow, expect this rivalry to grow with it.

games. Many of these fans were then banned from games without warning for not—in the team's words—"conforming to the values of PSG."

Some say this is PSG's way of trying to make its fans include only a certain kind of supporter—wealthy, or elite. Perhaps this is true. "If you can find a ticket to a PSG game nowadays, you're liable to be welcomed outside the Parc by jazz orchestras instead of skinheads," says Kuper. In addition, "The club's VIP salons and burgeoning luxury suites may boast more celebrities per square foot than any restaurant in Paris."

Not everyone is happy about this development and what they see as a shift in focus away from the pitch and toward the overall brand of the club. "What the club's leadership is doing is taking a popular, down-to-earth football [soccer] club and transforming it into a pack of laundry detergent," one longtime fan told the *New York Times*.

The team celebrates winning four competitions in 2015.

5 PARIS SAINT-GERMAIN: NOW AND IN THE FUTURE

Since its founding in 1970, Paris Saint-Germain has become incredibly successful. However, the team is just getting started, and it has plenty of time to grow into an even greater team.

THE MOST SUCCESSFUL CLUB IN FRENCH HISTORY

Paris Saint-Germain is without question the most successful club in French history. It has won more major titles than any other French team. Major titles are Ligue 1 championships, Ligue 2 championships, Coupes de France, Coupes de la Ligue, Trophées des Champions, and UEFA championships.

Since its promotion to Ligue 1 in 1975, PSG has never been relegated to Ligue 2. It is the only Ligue 1 team to never face relegation. Although the team was demoted to Division 3 after its split from Paris FC in 1972, this was for administrative rather than performance reasons, so it doesn't count as an official relegation. PSG has also played the most consecutive

The 2018 Paris Saint-Germain squad celebrates after winning the Coupe de France. Paris Saint-Germain has won this title more than any other French team.

seasons in Ligue 1 of any French club: forty-five as of 2018–2019. It's one of just two French clubs to have won an international title (the European Cup Winners' Cup in 1996). Also, it's the only squad to win all four national titles—Ligue 1, Coupe de France, Coupe de la Ligue, and the Trophées des Champions—in a single season. This accomplishment is called a quadruple. PSG has won a quadruple three times.

There's one record that has escaped PSG, and that is the record of most Ligue 1 titles. PSG has won seven. Association Sportive (AS) de Saint-Étienne has won ten. However, AS de Saint-Étienne started in 1919 and has played sixty-six seasons in Ligue 1. In contrast, PSG started in 1970 and has played just forty-five seasons in that league as of 2019. In other words, AS de Saint-Étienne has played twenty-one more Ligue 1 seasons than PSG but has won only three more titles. The last time AS de Saint-Étienne won a title was in 1980–1981. It may well be the case that PSG catches and even passes AS de Saint-Étienne in the near future.

THE NEXT GENERATION OF STARS

In recent years, PSG has signed several top athletes from around the world—players like Thiago Silva, Zlatan Ibrahimović, Edinson Cavani, David Beckham, David Luiz, Neymar, and Kylian Mbappé. These players were stars before they came to PSG. However, PSG doesn't just sign players who are already stars. The club also

Star soccer player David Beckham played for Paris Saint-Germain in 2013 before retiring from the game.

SPORT SHORT

Three 2018–2019 PSG players graduated from the PSG Academy: Adrien Rabiot, Alphonse Areola, and Presnel Kimpembe.

works to cultivate, or raise, the next crop of top young players. PSG organizes soccer teams, camps, and programs for children around the world to learn more about the game. It then invites the most promising young players to study, train, play for, and even live at its youth facility in France. This facility is called the Paris Saint-Germain Academy. There are 140 young players

A Paris Saint-Germain Academy camp takes place in Brooklyn, New York. Top players are asked to move to France to study at and play for the academy.

ages thirteen to nineteen enrolled at the PSG Academy as of 2019.

The PSG Academy opened in 1975. In 2016, the club committed to building a new academy, set to open in 2019. It features state-of-the-art classrooms, nine soccer fields (including one indoor field), fitness rooms and recovery areas, a medical treatment room, and a comfortable place for students to live in. By building a new academy, the club "has made its ambition abundantly clear: to give young talents the best possible chance to emerge, make progress, and shine," says the academy's website.

BECOMING A CHAMPIONS LEAGUE FIGHTER

PSG's success in France has been impressive, but PSG doesn't just want to be the best team in France. It wants to be the best team in all of Europe.

To become the best team in Europe, PSG must win the Champions League. However, as of 2019, PSG has never gone further in the Champions League tournament than the quarterfinals. Lately, it hasn't even made it that far. In 2018–2019, PSG lost to a team called Manchester United in the round of sixteen. This happened even though everyone thought PSG would win. This loss was very disappointing to PSG fans and players.

PSG lost to Manchester United, but it wasn't necessarily because Manchester United was the better team. Manchester United got a few lucky shots. Near the end of the game, the officials called a questionable

Kylian Mbappé of Paris Saint-Germain reacts to losing to Manchester United in the 2019 Champions League round of sixteen.

"hand ball" (meaning the ball hit a player's hand) against a PSG player. This gave Manchester United a penalty kick, which they scored. PSG lost the game and was out of the tournament.

However, there's good news. PSG has some of the world's top young players. If these players stick around and stay healthy, PSG may win the Champions League—and soon! In any case, it is likely to stay a top French soccer team for years to come.

CHRONOLOGY

1904 Stade Saint-Germain is started in a suburb outside Paris.

1957 Stade Saint-Germain wins the Division d'Honneur de la Ligue de Paris.

1969 Stade Saint-Germain reaches the quarterfinals in the Coupe de France, and Paris FC is founded.

1970 Paris FC merges with Stade Saint-Germain to form a new team called Paris Saint-Germain (PSG).

1971 PSG is promoted to Ligue 1.

1972 PSG splits into two teams: Paris FC and PSG, and PSG is demoted to Division 3.

1973–1974 PSG plays its first season in Parc des Princes.

1974 PSG returns to Ligue 1.

1982 PSG wins its first major trophy: the Coupe de France.

1984 PSG qualifies for the Europa League for the first time ever.

1995 PSG player George Weah wins the Ballon d'Or award.

1986 PSG wins Ligue 1 and qualifies for the Champions League for the first time ever.

1996 PSG wins its first international championship: the European Cup Winners' Cup.

2011 QSi buys PSG.

2014 PSG wins its first ever domestic quadruple—the first of three.

2017 PSG signs Neymar.

2018 PSG signs Kylian Mbappé.

GLOSSARY

amateur A person or team that is not professional.

criticize To express a negative opinion of something.

defender A player on a soccer team who plays closest to his or her team's goal. Defenders help the goalie protect the goal.

draw When two teams have the same score at the end of the allotted time. Another word for draw is tie.

final The last game in a tournament. The winner of the final wins the tournament.

forward A player on a soccer team who plays closest to the other team's goal. Forwards generally score more goals than players in other positions; also called striker.

goalie The player on a soccer team who protects the team's goal. Another word for goalie is goalkeeper.

hooligan An annoying and sometimes violent soccer fan.

kit Soccer uniform.

knockout tournament A tournament format in which the winner of the match advances to the next round and the loser is no longer in contention.

match A soccer game.

midfielder A player on a soccer team who plays in the middle of the field, between the team's forwards and defenders.

pitch The field on which a soccer match is played.

quarterfinal A game or round in a tournament immediately before the semifinal round.

relegation The demotion of a soccer club from one league to the league below it.

round-robin A tournament format in which every competitor plays every other competitor at least once.

semifinal A game or round in a tournament immediately before the final. The winners of a semifinal go on to play in the final.

sponsor A company or other organization that forms a relationship with a team. Typically, sponsors pay teams money to help support the team. In exchange, the team might put the sponsor's logo on its jerseys or near the field of play.

striker The player on a soccer team whose main job is to score goals. The striker typically plays at the center-forward position.

transfer fee A fee paid by a soccer club to get a player who is under contract with another club on their team. Transfer fees often cost a lot of money.

winger A player on a soccer team who plays along the side edges of the field.

FURTHER INFORMATION

BOOKS

Fishman, Jon M. *Neymar.* Minneapolis, MN: LernerClassroom, 2018.

Gifford, Clive. *The Ultimate Champions League Fan Guide.* London, UK: Carlton Kids, 2018.

Kortemeier, Todd. *Kylian Mbappé.* Mendota Heights, MN: Focus Readers, 2019.

Stewart, Mark. *Paris Saint-Germain.* Chicago, IL: Norwood House Press, 2017.

WEBSITES

Ligue 1

https://www.ligue1.com

This is the official English-language Ligue 1 website.

Paris Saint-Germain Football Club

https://en.psg.fr

This is the official English-language Paris Saint-Germain website.

Soccer24.com

https://www.soccer24.com/france/ligue-1

Stay on top of Ligue 1, Ligue 2, Coupe de France, and other action on this website.

UEFA Champions League

https://www.uefa.com/uefachampionsleague/index.html

Get the latest news about the Champions League here.

VIDEOS

Kylian Mbappé Highlights 2018/19

https://www.youtube.com/watch?v=uLD5FJPEJ04

This video shows a series of top goals and other plays by Kylian Mbappé during the 2018–2019 season.

Paris Saint-Germain: Football Clubs in 2 Minutes

https://www.youtube.com/watch?v=Nm5UY9qE-eM

Watch PSG footage past and present—set to a popular song that celebrates PSG—in this video.

Paris Saint-Germain Top 30 Goals 2017/2018

https://www.youtube.com/watch?v=-12LvCDqVos

This video contains a compilation of the top thirty goals scored by PSG during the 2017–2018 season.

SELECTED BIBLIOGRAPHY

Ahmed, Murad. "PSG 'Overstated' Sponsorships Valued at €200 Million, Says UEFA Probe." FT.com. April 11, 2018. Accessed March 29, 2019. https://www.ft.com/content/004c9d5e-3cdc-11e8-b7e0-52972418fec4.

Bairner, Robin. "Monaco Star Mbappe Completes €180 Million Paris Saint-Germain Move." Goal.com. August 31, 2017. Accessed March 28, 2019. https://www.goal.com/en/news/monaco-star-mbappe-completes-180-million-paris-saint-germain/13k7x4cozao191hcdgpw1kkrrt.

Borden, Sam. "A League of One." *New York Times*. March 6, 2013. Accessed March 29, 2019. https://www.nytimes.com/2013/03/07/sports/soccer/in-france-paris-st-germain-is-a-league-apart.html.

Bryan-Low, Cassell, and Tom Bergin. "The Money Game: How Top Soccer Clubs Clashed with Rules on Financial Fair Play." Reuters.com. November 2, 2018. Accessed March 29, 2019. https://www.reuters.com/investigates/special-report/soccer-files-fairplay.

"The Business of Soccer: The List." *Forbes*. 2019. Accessed March 29, 2019. https://www.forbes.com/soccer-valuations/list/#tab:overall.

Caley, Michael. "It Might Finally Be Someone Else's Turn in the Champions League." March 4, 2019. *Five Thirty Eight*. Accessed March 30, 2019. https://fivethirtyeight.com/features/it-might-finally-be-someone-elses-turn-in-the-champions-league.

Conn, David. "Paris Saint-Germain May Face UEFA Sanctions for Over-Valued Qatari Deals." *Guardian*. April 11, 2018. Accessed March 30, 2019. https://www.theguardian.com/football/2018/apr/11/psg-may-face-uefa-sanctions-overvalued-qatari-deal.

"Football in France and the Significance of World War I." WorldSoccer.com. December 6, 2014. Accessed March 27, 2019. https://www.worldsoccer.com/blogs/football-france-significance-world-war-1-358236.

Fortescue, William. *The Third Republic in France, 1870-1940.* London, UK: Routledge, 2017.

"Histoire du Paris Saint-Germain Football Club." Accessed March 27, 2019. http://psg70.free.fr/historique.htm.

Johnson, Jonathan. "Why the Return of Paris Saint-Germain's Ultras Is Such a Big Deal." ESPN. November 12, 2016. Accessed March 29, 2019. http://www.espn.com/soccer/club/paris-saint-germain/160/blog/post/2994952/why-the-return-of-paris-saint-germains-ultras-is-such-a-big-deal.

Kuper, Simon. "Can Paris Saint-Germain Become the World's Richest Sports Club?" FT.com. March 28, 2014. Accessed March 28, 2019. https://www.ft.com/content/ae88a0b2-b53a-11e3-af92-00144feabdc0.

Leadbetter, Sam. "How PSG Lost Its Soul." Look Left Online. December 1, 2013. Accessed March 29, 2019. https://www.lookleftonline.org/2013/12/how-psg-lost-its-soul.

"Le Stade Saint-Germanois, L'Ancetre du PSG (1904-1970)." PSGFC. 2017. Accessed March 27, 2019. http://www.psgfc.fr/le-psg/du-stade-saint-germain-au-paris-saint-germain-fc.

McMahon, Bobby. "Why Paris Saint-Germain's Financial Statements Qualify as Fiction." *Forbes*. July 21, 2013. Accessed March 29, 2019. https://www.forbes.com/sites/bobbymcmahon/2013/07/21/why-paris-saint-germains-financial-statements-qualify-as-fiction/#7c8df798770e.

Newman, Liam. "A World of Ultras: Marseille." *Football Times*. October 15, 2014. Accessed March 28, 2019. https://thesefootballtimes.co/2014/10/15/a-world-of-ultras-marseille.

Sayare, Scott. "Qatar Is Becoming a Player in French Sports." *New York Times*. October 26, 2012. Accessed March 30, 2019. https://www.nytimes.com/2012/10/27/sports/soccer/with-paris-saint-germain-qatar-is-a-player-in-french-sports.html.

Schofield, Hugh. "PSG's Dramatic Rise to European Giants." *Forbes*. May 8, 2014. Accessed March 29, 2019. https://www.bbc.com/news/world-europe-27314338.

Shea, Alexander. "The Last of the Ultras: Paris Saint-Germain and the Repression of Football Fans in France." *Football Times*. February 28, 2018. Accessed March 29, 2019. https://thesefootballtimes.co/2018/02/28/the-last-of-the-ultras-psg-and-the-repression-of-football-fans-in-france.

Skiver, Kevin. "PSG's Collapse Against Manchester United Is the Club's Latest Champions League Disappointment." CBSSports. March 6, 2019. Accessed March 30, 2019. https://www.cbssports.com/soccer/news/psgs-collapse-against-manchester-united-is-the-clubs-latest-champions-league-disappointment.

INDEX

Page numbers in **boldface** are images.

ABOUT THE AUTHOR

Kate Shoup has written more than forty books and has edited hundreds more. When not working, Shoup loves to travel, watch IndyCar racing, ski, read, and ride her motorcycle. She lives in Indianapolis with her husband and their dog.